When collecting art first became fashionable in the 17th century, it was customary to make family collections accessible to interested parties. My family is a follower of this practice and we welcome visitors who come to look at the Six collection. Always housed in Amsterdam, the collection was first located at no. 619 Herengracht, before moving to 509-511 at the end of the 18th century, and finally round the corner to its present location at 218 Amstel in 1915.

Through marriage over the generations, the original Six collection has been enlarged and enriched by a number of legacies - most notably from Margaretha Tulp, daughter of Dr Nicolaes Tulp, who was the subject of Rembrandt's famous 'Anatomy Lesson'. From the Hop family, creators of *Haagse Hopjes*, one of Holland's national sweets, came our marvellous silver treasures. Lucretia van Winter contributed the large correspondence archive of her grandparents, along with her own collecting and literary passions, and the house has been further enhanced by the contributions of the Teding van Berkhout and Bosch Reitz families.

The history of our art collection is rich and colourful. Each of the paintings on display has a history, representing an integral piece of my family's heritage and history. As you read the story of these treasures, which link the past so graphically to the present, I hope you will come to appreciate why I have written this booklet from my own perspective.

The Six collection existed long before I did, and will - I hope - be maintained for many more generations. It gives me tremendous pleasure to offer you this impression of the House of Six, our home.

Jan Six van Hillegom

Hall at the entrance with 17th, 18th and 19th century Dutch tiles

Amstel 218, from across the river Amstel

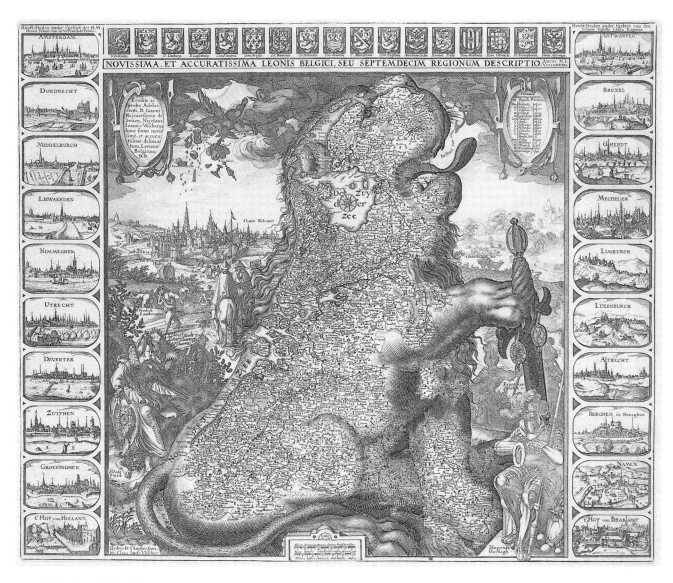

The Republic of the Netherlands, a so-called Leo-map, by Claes Jansz. Visscher

THE STORY OF SIX

In his book *Histoire de Chambray et du Cambresis* (published in Leiden in 1664) Jean le Carpentier traces the roots of our family back to the 12th century. He does so on the basis of a large number of charters and documents describing the Cambresis region and the Six family in particular. The earliest mention of our family name is to be found on a charter in the Abbey of Saint André, dated 1080. It refers to Landry Six, the 'Chevalier Chatelain' of Cambresis castle, married to Closcende, sister of Watier Turpin. Le Carpentier traces several other members of the Six family, including Hugues, Simon, Jean, Guillaume and Alexandre, who lived in the Duchy of Artois over the ensuing decades. Although the Duchy formed part of the Netherlands, it fell under the rule of King Philip II of Spain during the 16th century. The commanding officer of the Spanish army at the time was the infamous Duke of Alva.

< Chrétienne Six, by Cornelis Ketel, 1615

The foundations of the Republic of the Netherlands were laid by William of Orange between 1580 and 1584. The turbulent times and the excessive distance between the Six family business - a cloth weaving mill - and its customers, made a move inevitable. In 1586, Charles Six, married to Alix de Lattre in Saint Omer, moved his wife, their children Chrétienne, Jean and Guillaume and the weaving business to Amsterdam, an up-and-coming metropolis in the north of the Republic of the Netherlands.

In 1606, one of Charles's sons - Jean - married Anna Wymer. Her family not only originated from the Artois region, it was also actively involved in the cloth industry. Anna and Jean resided at 'de Blauwe Arend', today 103 Kloveniersburgwal in Amsterdam, and had two sons, Pieter and Jan.

A cloth seal made of lead from the dyeing factory of Charles Six, 'gheverft te amsterdam door charles six van armentier, 1589'

Saint Omer, early 17th century

The name Jan is a Dutch translation of Jean. As such, I am the tenth generation of Jan Six. To make this booklet more readable, I will not always refer to my early ancestors in terms of 'great great, etc. grandfather or grandmother'. To give you an example of why I have chosen this approach, Jan Six I is my great-great-great-great-great-great-great-great grandfather. For full details, please see the family tree on pages 34 and 35.

In 1655, Jan Six I married Margaretha Tulp, daughter of the famous surgeon Nicolaes Tulp, who would later become Mayor of Amsterdam. Jan Six had little interest in the family business, which was run by his brother Pieter. Instead, Jan was drawn to the world of art and culture and between 1639 and 1641 he took himself on a Grand Tour of Italy. Jan proved to be a highly capable writer of essays, poetry and plays.
He was a member of the so-called 'Muiderkring', a fraternity that included well-known Dutch writers and poets like Pieter Cornelisz. Hooft and Joost van den Vondel. In addition, he held the position of Governor of Amsterdam on a number of occasions, even becoming its Mayor for a brief period in 1691.

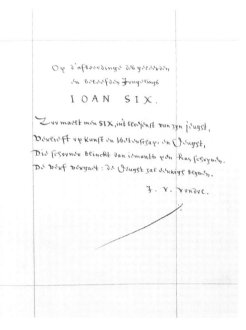

Jan Six I maintained close and friendly relations with a variety of painters, including Rembrandt van Rijn, who painted Jan's portrait in 1654, having produced a number of etchings and drawings of and for him from 1645 onwards. These works of art form the basis of the present Six collection.

Owing to a series of acquisitions and marriages and the levying of death duties, the composition of the Six collection has changed over the generations. But its core series of family portraits has remained intact.

THE HOUSE OF SIX

Although the premises situated at 218 Amstel date back to about 1664, they were not occupied by the Six family until 1915. In fact, the house was acquired by my great grandfather - Jan Six VII - and his wife Hieronyma Maria Anthonia Fortunata Bosch Reitz in 1914. During that year our family house at 509-511 Herengracht was expropriated and demolished to enable the Vijzelstraat to be widened.

Large sections of the Herengracht interior were moved and installed in their entirety. Among them the doors to the conservatory and several of the trompe l'oeil panels known as 'Witjes', including those produced by Jacob de Wit, along with a polychromous painting dating back to 1752 and the grey and red grisaille by Taco Jelgersma. The entire side room ceiling was also moved.

Moving to the family's new premises, from Herengracht to Amstel in 1915

<< Jan Six I standing at the window Two studies, sepia drawing and pencil drawing, the copperplate and etching, all by Rembrandt van Rijn, 1647

The Amstel premises were extensively refurbished in 1726, when an additional floor, a lavatory column and a large outhouse were added. The stucco decorations by Ignatius van Lochteren, which adorn the ceiling in the hallways and the stairwell, were also added at that time.

< Drawing 'Homer reciting his verses', by Rembrandt van Rijn and a poem by Joost van den Vondel, both part of Jan Six I's Album Amicorum named 'Pandora', 1652

THE DRAWING ROOM

Two family portraits guard the entrance to the drawing room, the first being one of the earliest of our family portraits, painted in 1615 by C. Ketel. The painting shows Chrétienne Six, wife to Dr Nicholaes Mulerius.
The second painting, made by Pieter Saenredam in 1654, depicts the Parish church (*Buurtkerk*) in Utrecht, an exquisite example of Saenredam's masterful painting of churches.

Jan Six I's prosperous career owed much to his marriage to Margaretha Tulp, daughter of Dr Nicolaes Tulp. One of the nine portraits of Dr Tulp on display was painted by Jurriaen Ovens in 1658.
Tulp was - and remains - one of Amsterdam's most famous citizens. He started his career as a doctor, progressing to become professor of anatomy and, at a later stage in life, Mayor of Amsterdam. The companion portrait, to the other side of the chimney, is of his second wife, Margaretha de Vlaming van Oudshoorn. It was painted by Dirck Santvoort.

Below the portrait of Dr Nicolaes Tulp is a painting of his son Diederick and Diederick's second wife, Catharine Resteau de Beaufort, daughter of the renowned banker. These paintings are by Caspar Netscher. Left of this painting hang two portraits by Dirck Santvoort of Dirck Vries (1603-1641) and Maria Dorhouts (1619-?). The latter painting also depicts Jan and Elisabeth van den Bempden-Tulp.

'The Parish church' (Buurtkerk) in Utrecht, by Pieter Saenredam, 1654

< The Drawing room

Beneath the portrait of Margaretha de Vlaming van Oudshoorn is a painting by Gerrit Berckheyde, dated 1672. It is entitled 'Bend in Herengracht' (*Bocht in de Herengracht*) and shows the well-known stretch of the Herengracht leading up to the Spiegelstraat. In an attempt to prove that Amsterdam was every bit as pretty as Venice (a message amplified by a poem on the back of the painting) Berckheyde deliberately left out the trees lining the Herengracht. In those days, Venice was also known as the 'Pearl of Europe'. The cat on the table was painted by Henriëtte Ronner-Knip.

The door at the far side of the drawing room opens up to a balcony with a chimney piece featuring a wonderful variety

'Bend in Herengracht' (Bocht in de Herengracht), by Gerrit Berckheyde, 1672

of sea shells. Prior to a renovation carried out at the beginning of the 20th century, the present balcony served as a conservatory. Its conversion affords us a direct view of the garden and the nearly 200 year old male Ginko Biloba tree, situated to the side of the balcony.

> Louis XV 'Master Cabinet' (Meesterkastje)

The Louis XV Master Cabinet 'en miniature' (*Meesterkastje*) between the windows dates back to around 1740. The cabinet is typical of those made by apprentice cabinetmakers, keen to demonstrate their abilities to the guild of which they formed part. If the masters of the guild approved of the cabinet's build, quality and overall feel, the apprentice would himself be promoted to master cabinetmaker.

The sink cat on the table was painted by Henriëtte Ronner-Knip.

The gardens were last renovated in 1989. The aim was - and is - to reintroduce the ambience of 17th century landscape architecture, for exam-ple by placing terracotta statues of 'Venus' and 'Neptune' by Daniël Marot. The outbuilding, which carries the name 'Heilust', was constructed by Jan Six VII's children to show him that they had mastered a trade. 'Heilust' has an interesting history of its own.

It was actually constructed at 'Jagtlust' in 's-Graveland, the former family's summer residence. It remained there until 1993, when it was partially restored by the former head gardener at 'Jagtlust' and moved to its present location.

The watercolour painting between the second set of windows shows the Church of St. Anne's (*Annakerk*) in Haarlem. It was painted by Pieter Saenredam, whose oil painting of the same church is on view at the Museum of Fine Arts in Budapest. The small round panel entitled 'He who can straighten that which is bent or crooked, is fit to wear the red scarlet' (*Hij die het kromme regt kan maken, die mag dragen het rood scharlaken*) was painted by Pieter Breughel the Elder. Breughel intended it to be a satire on the legal establishment in the late 16th century.

'He who can straighten that which is bent or crooked, is fit to wear the red scarlet'
(Hij die het kromme regt kan maken, die mag dragen het rood scharlaken),
'The Lawyer', by Pieter Breughel, ca. 1590

To the side of the conservatory doors are two portraits by Lucas van Leyden dating back to around 1525. The uppermost of these is most likely a self-portrait.

The gardens with the outbuilding, 'Heilust'

The two octagonal paintings by Thomas de Keyzer were, in fact, signed by Gerard Dou, presumably because it was felt that the Master's signature would make the paintings more valuable. Last, but not least, is a painting by Rachel Ruysch entitled 'Geranium', the first of her paintings to receive public acclaim.

The Empire room

THE EMPIRE ROOM

Most of the Empire room was moved from the Herengracht in its entirety; its contents probably date back to around 1820, and offer an excellent example of what a family collection actually means. Many of the items on display can be found in the paintings adorning the walls. These include the harp, the aigrette, the inkstand and the modern-day descendent of the camellia plant, which spends its winters hibernating in the conservatory. The portrait of Lucretia Six-van Winter by A.J. Dubois Drahonet, which was painted in 1825, shows several of these items. Her husband, Hendrik Six, of whom Dubois Drahonet also painted a portrait, was a keen botanist. In fact, he was the first botanist in Europe to import the camellia plant, which is shown in the painting, from its native Japan (1823). Hendrik was ennobled in 1841.

The empire room also features a portrait of Maria Susanna Teding van Berkhout-van Collen, painted by A. de Lelie in 1792. The drape that half covers the por-trait of her husband indicates that Maria was a widow at the time. The robe would be partially or entirely removed once the mourning period was over. On close observation, the silver inkstand which still stands on the table right below the painting, can also be discerned. To the right of Maria's portrait is Jan Kruseman's painting of Pieter Jacob Teding van Berkhout. It was painted around 1847.

Hendrik Six and Lucretia Six-van Winter, by A.J. Dubois Drahonet, 1825; a flower from the first camellia plant, imported from Japan (1823); a miniature portrait of Jan Six VI as a baby and the aigrette with ostrich feathers.

Pieter van Winter and Anna Louise van der Poorten, by J.F.A. Tischbein, ca. 1794

Pieter was Maria's grandson. The companion portrait, above the piano-forte, was also painted by Kruseman and depicts Pieter's wife Hieronyma Maria Anthonia Fortunata van Slingelandt. To the left of the mantelpiece you will see two portaits by J.F.A. Tischbein. They show Pieter van Winter and his wife Anna Louise van der Poorten. To the right of the mantelpiece are portraits of Pieter van Winter, painted by Adriaen de Lelie and of Joshua van Winter, painted by A.J. Dubois Drahonet. The design of the clock on the mantelpiece, which carries the name 'Le Porte-fait', was inspired by a French novel entitled 'Paul et Virginie' (1788).

Its author, Bernardin de St. Pierre, urged his readers to change their lifestyle and to steer away from materialism towards a state of being at one with nature, not unlike the Negroes described in 'Le Bon Sauvage'.

The clock on the mantelpiece, 'Le Portefait'

Kang H'si and Kraak porcelain, collected during the end of the 18th century. On both sides silhouettes of family members, made at the end of the 19th century.

Delft white elephant, signed J.H., 17th century

The Chinese black lacquered six-fold screen and Japanese furniture which adorn the room were highly fashionable in the 1820's, the black upholstery is made from horsetail hairs.

The show case contains Kang H'si porcelain (1662-1722).
The Delft white elephant, signed 'J.H.' on the stove (probably 17th century) is one of my favourites.

THE POTTER ROOM

The Potter room was constructed in 1915 on top of the indoor stables, to house the striking portrait of Diederick Tulp on horseback, painted in 1653. However, on completion it was discovered that the room was too small. Although the size of the painting had been calculated correctly, no account had been taken of the frame. To remedy the situation, approximately 7 centimetres of the neighbour's inner courtyard were acquired, allowing the room to be widened and the painting to be hung. In former days, the room was mostly used by servants waiting on the dining

Diederick Tulp, by Paulus Potter, 1653 (after restoration in 1995)

< The Potter room with the unrestored painting by Paulus Potter, seen from the dining room

15

congregation. The furnishings and fittings, particularly the wallpaper and the false doors, were derived from the Six residence at the Herengracht.

The Potter room also houses a painting by Nicolaes Eliasz. Pickenoy, dating back to 1624. The painting is entitled 'The Game of Golf' (*Het Golfspel*) and suggests that the sport of golf may have originated in the Netherlands (a view I will make no attempt to uphold here). The carriage painted in the background belonged to Nicolaes Tulp and is worthy of special notice by virtue of its four wheels. In the early to mid 1600's, there was a fear in Amsterdam that the reverberations of carriage wheels would cause houses to become dislodged from the wooden piles on which they had been constructed. As a result, wheeled carriages were forbidden. Carriages used slide plates instead, not unlike the runners used on sleds. Although the slide plates were greased to reduce friction, they made for slow transportation, which, in turn, reduced the number of road accidents. However, as head of one of the largest medical practices in Amsterdam, Nicolaes Tulp was often required to attend to patients at short notice. As a result, he was one of a few citizens permitted to use a wheeled carriage.

The Game of Golf (Het Golfspel), by Nicolaes Eliasz. Pickenoy, 1624

The painting itself depicts a number of people, including Nicolaes Tulp's mother, Gherytgen van Poelenburg, and her three grandchildren from Tulp's first marriage (Pieter, Egbert and Catharina).

The painting on the opposite wall is also by Nicolaes Eliasz. Pickenoy and is dated 1636. The figure to the left is Tulp's son Diederick. The girl wearing the yellow dress is Tulp's youngest daughter Margaretha, who would later marry Jan Six. Diederick Tulp had no relatives other than his granddaughter, who would later marry Jan Six II. As a result of these two marriages, the entire Tulp legacy became part of the Six collection.

This inheritance included two Limoges enamels, by Jean II Penigaud, dating back to the 16th century. They show the 'Entering Jerusalem' (*Intocht in Jerusalem*) and 'The Birth' (*De Geboorte*). The 17th century footstoves in front of the Potter painting were used in church. The modelled clay Satyr group is by Arthus Quellinus, probably as a study.

Dr Nicolaes Tulp and his family, by Nicolaes Eliasz. Pickenoy, 1636

THE INNER ROOM

The gold-coloured wallcovering in the Inner room, commissioned by Diederick Tulp in 1683 for his country estate 'Tulpenburg', was made by Flemish leathermaker Caspar Reytz in approximately 1680. Until 1750, this type of wall covering, which is made of wild boar leather, was given its texture by the pressing of engraved metal plates onto wet leather. Once dried, the leather would be coloured and gilded by hand. The wall covering in the Inner room uses two different plates.
On the portrait of Jan van den Bempden by Carel de Moor, three heads are visible at the bottom right of the covering and represent the three Roman gods Mars (war), Apollo (music) and Mercury (trade). By pointing to himself with one hand and to the three gods with the other, Jan seems to indicate that he is 'just like them'.

< Jodocus van den Bempden, by Ferdinand Bol, 1659, in the gilded leather covered Inner Room

Ten dancing putti, by Jacopo di Palma the younger, ca. 1580

The painting of dancing putti by Jacopo di Palma the younger shows two girls joining in the fun. Strictly speaking, putti are always masculine. Below is a portrait of Jodocus van den Bempden by Ferdinand Bol, dated 1659. Perhaps a little morbid, we refer to it as 'the dead little uncle'. Many of the symbols depicted in the painting indicate that Jodocus has passed away. These include the extinguished torch, the wilted rose (shown as little more than a bud), the setting sun and the blossoming flowers surrounding the soul. Next to the portrait of Jodocus hangs a painting by Thérèse Schwartze (1910) of a dead child from the Teding van Berkhout family. This portrait does not indulge in symbolism, but relies instead on the child's folded hands to convey a strong sense of faith.

The show case contains the pink 18th century 'Famille Rose' china, each item of which has been decorated with a yellow flower. The 19th century chess-set features a slightly odd white king piece, which we nicknamed 'the Napoleon with the Chinese eyes'. Whoever he might be, his opposite number is the infamous Genghis Khan.

The briefcase, which belonged to Jan Six II, is made of Persian leather with gold embroidery. The large painting by A.C. Beeldemaker (1666) shows Nicolaes Tulp and his granddaughter Margaretha, child of Catharina Tulp and Arent Tholinx. They lived next-door to Nicolaes on the Keizersgracht. In the 17th century small details often refer to a symbolic matter: the six apples, held by Margaretha, from the tree behind her and could be seen as a symbol of the six grandchildren of Nicolaes Tulp at that time and his posterity in general.

Chess men, Napoleon and Genghis Khan, ca. 1810

THE DINING ROOM

Between 1928 and 1934 the size of the collection was reduced considerably. Not only did my great-grandfather - Jan Six VII - have to buy out his brother Willem, he also faced death duties. In 1922 the Six Foundation was created. Among the paintings to leave the collection were Johannes Vermeer's 'The Street' (*Het Straatje*) and 'The Milkmaid' (*Het Melkmeisje*), which were sold in 1928 and 1932 respectively.

The dining room hosts a large number of prominent paintings, among them Jacob Ruysdael's 'Landscape Featuring Mountain Torrent' (*Landschap met bergstroom*). Like Albert Cuyp, Ruysdael painted landscapes mostly from his imagination, although he would occasionally refer to sketches produced by his friend Everdingen, who regularly visited Sweden.

The paintings by Cornelis Troost, entitled 'Indecent Love' (*Wanhebbelijke Liefde*) depict scenes from a play. To the right, a lecher is robbed of his wallet, much to the amusement of the man in the background of the painting. Although the young man shown to the left appears to fall for the old frump's advances, the handmaiden standing in the doorway fathoms the situation correctly. Both paintings contain a beach scene, a symbolic warning against a ship-wrecked marriage. Albert Cuyp's 'Landscape by Moonlight' (*Landschap bij Maanlicht*) is rather unusual given his preference for highly-lit scenes featuring cows. The pendent, entitled 'Rough Seas during Daytime' (*Ruwe zee bij dag*), is on show at the Louvre in Paris.

< 'Landscape by Moon-light' (Landschap bij Maanlicht), by Albert Cuyp above a Dutch buffet dated around 1775

The dining table, dressed for a private party

The silver soup terrines, by Engelbach Joosten were given by the State of Holland to Mr Johannes Hop resigning as Counsellor and Chief Treasurer in 1769.

The Egyptian priest, Nswj basalt, ca. 1700 BC

Glass cabinet with miniature silver toys, flanked by portraits of Nicolaes Tulp by Nicolaes Eliasz. Pickenoy (right) and Jan Six VI by August Allebé Above, William of Orange Nassau and his wife Louise de Coligny by Michiel van Miereveld, and the Amstelhouse by Berckheyde, 1685

The two sideboards on either side of the chimney are typical Dutch furniture (so-called 'Klapbuffet'). The rear folds away to enable the lady of the house to wash up the precious Chinese tea set. Despite the servants, eight of whom lived in the house itself, this delicate task remained her prerogative. View of the Amstel' (*Gezicht op de Amstel*) was painted by Gerrit Berckheyde in 1685. The painting shows Amstel 216 and 218 and was acquired during the early part of the 20th century. To the right on the painting the white house was designed by Adriaen Dortsman (1685). The house was inhabited by Mr van Beuningen, the Mayor of Amsterdam. The Mayor's boat is clearly visible. Allegedly van Beuningen went mad later in life, and used his own blood to write his name on the building's façade. His and other names (alongside drawings of ships and other mysterious markings) can still be seen there. Notable for its absence is the 'Skinny bridge' (*Magere brug*), which was not built until 1691. The glass cabinet contains 17th and 18th century silver toys.

The dining room also houses portraits of William of Orange and Louise de Coligny by Michiel van Mierevelt. When commissioned to paint a portrait, van Mierevelt was often asked to make a number of copies at the same time.

The portrait of Jan Six VI, who was an avid coin collector, is by August Allebé.

The portrait of Nicolaes Tulp by Frans Hals dates back to 1644. The portrait is very rare in that few of Hals' subjects are actually known by name. Just below the painting is a 2,250-year-old Egyptian statue of Nswj . The painting entitled 'Fun fair at Rijswijk' (*Kermis te Rijswijk*) was painted by Esaias van de Velde in 1625. The painting was originally commissioned by the leading citizens of Rijswijk, who are shown in the centre of the painting looking fairly pleased with themselves. Also shown are their guests, the princes Maurits and Frederik Hendrik and the King and Queen of Bohemia. Unfortunately, the notables refused to pay for the painting and Van der Velde clearly felt cheated. When the original frame was removed at the end of the last century, it was discovered that a defecating man was hidden under the left upright.

Jan Six VI, by August Allebé, 1882

'Fun fair at Rijswijk', by Esaias van de Velde, 1625

Jan Six III as a baby, by Jacob de Wet, ca. 1693

In the centre of the room above the dining table, the decoration halfway up the pole with the crown is an ostrich egg. In the 17th century, ostrich eggs were considered a status symbol. The Indian silk embroidered tablecloth and large carpet are both from about 1810.

To the right of the cabinet containing a large Meissen porcelain coffee and tea set are portraits of Jan Six II (by Jacob de Wet), Willem Six as a young hunter (by Nicolaes Maes) and Jan Six III as a baby wearing an Indian chief's headgear. Hanging to the left and right of the doorway are portraits of Diederick Tulp and his first wife Anna Burgh. Both were painted by Jurriaen Ovens in 1658.

< Nicolaes Tulp, by Frans Hals, 1644

Anna Six-Wymer, by Rembrandt van Rijn, 1641

THE SIDE ROOM

All the woodwork in the side room was derived from the Herengracht residence. The ceiling was moved in square blocks and a unique solution was found for the door. Standing in the side room, you won't notice that the door is too wide. Conversely, if you are standing in the hallway, you won't notice the single door. The two-doors-in-one solution allowed the symmetry of the Louis XVI room to be retained. As is typical of the Louis XVI style, the side room contains many gold-coloured items.

The portrait of Anna Wymer was painted by Rembrandt van Rijn in 1641. The difference between the restrained style of this painting and the more exuberant and impressionistic style of the painting of Jan Six I does not lie in the master's age (35) or his professional development as a painter. It reflects the fact that the painting was commissioned by Jan Six's mother, who, in keeping with custom, wanted the end result to be refined, modest and sober.

The portrait of Jan Six I was painted by Rembrandt in 1654. Experts have pronounced it the most beautiful ever painted by the master. The lively and very human painting represents one of the very rare occasions when Rembrandt allowed his own style to shine through, rather than forcing himself to be governed by contemporary customs and tastes. This 'impressionist' brush, together with the distinct colour red and the contrast in light are the three main features that Rembrandt's work is famous for, and all are strongly represented in this painting. Despite their very different backgrounds, Rembrandt - then 48 - and Jan Six - then 36 - were good friends. It has been suggested that the painting expresses the bond between them; both men supported the Renaissance ideal that noblemen should radiate their inner convictions by conducting themselves in an effortless and graceful manner. This explains why the painting is neither artificial nor indirect. Indeed, the painting shows Jan Six as a true nobleman and Rembrandt as a true painter of noblemen, a worthy heir to Titian, Raphael and Caravaggio.

The portrait painted on the inside of the golden box is of Jan Six I and Chloris, by the hand of Gerard Ter Borch. There is a remarkable resemblance between Chloris and Jan's future wife, Margaretha Tulp. It is nevertheless remarkable that her portrait should have remained hidden behind shellac until some time around 1825.

Jan Six I and 'Chloris', by Gerard Ter Borch, 1645?, painted on the inside of a golden box

The modest portrait of Margaretha Tulp was painted by Govert Flinck in 1656 showing Margaretha as a newly wed, expecting her first child, Anna. In all, Jan Six I and Margaretha had 11 children, 7 suffered cot death and 2 passed away before reaching adulthood. In fact, only two children, Jan II and Nicolaas, survived their parents.

Jan Six I, sepia drawing, study for the oil painting, by Rembrandt van Rijn, 1654

Margaretha Tulp expecting her first child, Anna, by Govert Flink, 1656

> Jan Six I, son of the last Jean Six, by Rembrandt van Rijn, 1654

Elisabeth van der Wolff bearing her embroidered gloves, by Michiel van Miereveldt, 1612

The wedding portraits of Robbert van der Hoeve and Elisabeth van der Wolff were painted by Michiel van Mierevelt in 1613. In the early 17th century it was customary for brides to wear black wedding gowns (white wedding gowns didn't become fashionable until the second half of the 20th century) and the wedding ring was worn around the right index finger, from where, it was believed, a vital artery ran directly to the heart. Elisabeth holds a pair of wedding gloves in her left hand. Its cuffs lie on the table, face down, just below the portrait. The chain around Elisabeth's waist - a traditional wedding present - is used to hang the keys to the house. Elisabeth died giving birth at the age of 20.

'The Church of St Lawrence' (Laurenskerk), by Antoine de Lorme, 1657

The painting by Antoine de Lorme, with figures added by Palamedes, shows the inside of the church of St Lawrence (*Laurenskerk*) in Rotterdam. The portraits left and right of the mantelpiece show Jan Six VII and Nine (H.M.A.F) Bosch Reitz. Both were painted by Jan Veth. The painting over the door is by Jacob de Wit and depicts Apollo.

Jan Six VII and his wife Hieronyma Maria Anthonia Fortunata (Nine) Bosch Reitz, by Jan Veth, 1901

THE HALLWAY

The main entrance is only opened when a member of the family marries or dies. The portraits near the front door show Jan Six III and Maria Jacoba Six (both children of Jan Six II), painted by A. Boonen. Between the doors are portraits of Jan Six II with two of his wives and his daughter painted by Boonen in 1714.

Jan Six II and his third wife Anna Elisabeth van den Bempden, by Arnold Boonen, 1714 and 1728

The portrait of Jan Six II's second wife, Maria Calkoen, can be seen to the side of Neptune. The Six family owes its continued existence to Jan Six II's third wife and niece Anna Elisabeth van den Bempden, who, following the death of Jan Six III, gave birth to a new Jan Six III in 1730. Her portrait, painted in 1728 by Arnold Boonen, hangs directly opposite that of Jan Six II.

Directly above the dollhouse you can see a portrait of Jan Six I by Wallerant Vaillant (1649), a completely different interpretation of Jan Six I to the one by Rembrandt six years later. The portrait opposite, is of Margaretha Tulp by Jurriaen Ovens 1658. As in all other paintings of Margaretha, she holds a small bouquet of flowers in her hand.

Jan Six I, by Wallerant Vaillant, 1649

< Jan Six III, by D. van der Smissen, ca.1765

Dr Nicolaes Tulp, by Arthus Quellinus, 1658 In the background Diogenes

17th century glasses: (from left to right) diamond-engraved glasses by Wolff, Greenwood, Sang, a mill-cup and a Duc d'Alve

The hallway also houses an ebony and marble tric-trac game with a porphyry ornamental pot beside it. The two marble busts - of Diogenes and Seneca - were produced in Italy during the late 17th century, while the Greek marble bust is that of Dr Nicolaes Tulp, made by Arthus Quellinus in 1658.

You could spend hours looking at the contents of the display cabinet. The glasswork to the left is mostly Venetian and dates back to the 17th century. An interesting feature is the flute-glass. As such, it wasn't used to drink champagne. This distinctly French invention wasn't available until the end of the 19th century. Instead, the flute-glass was a device that enabled those wearing a ruff to drink at all. Just below it you will find glassware of Dutch manufacture (Berkemeyers and Roemers - 16th and 17th century respectively). The engraved glasses are by Greenwood, Sang and Wolff.

Jan Six I's souvenir from his Grand Tour to Italy from 1639 to 1641, a massive Jaspis bowl fitted in enameled gold and its gold embossed basket

Just below it is a collection of Egyptian artefacts and a so-called 'Jack in the Cellar' (*Hansje in de Kelder*). This peculiar object has a history of its own. During the Golden Age, the 'Jack in the Cellar', in essence a silver bowl, was placed on the table to inform the guests that a child was on its way. A little float with a small baby on top sat halfway up the bowl and by filling the bowl with wine, the 'Jack in the Cellar' sneaked through an opening at the top of the bowl, indicating that a new life would soon grace the world. Guests would toast to the health of the unborn child and drink the wine in one large gulp. Other historical cups are a mill-glass and a so-called 'Spinolacup'. The central cabinet contains (top) a red ribbon, which was worn by the Mayor of Amsterdam during the execution of a convicted criminal. The Jaspis bowl is a souvenir brought back by Jan Six I from his Grand Tour of Italy.

17th century cups: (from left to right) 'Jack in the Cellar' (Hansje in de kelder), a 'Pineapple-cup', a 'Nautilus-cup', a 'Coconut-cup' and a silver and gold 'Spinolacup', holding a Roemer

Gilded silver 'Tulip cup', made by Johannes Lutma, 1652, commissioned by Dr Nicolaes Tulp as a present to the Surgeon Guild on his leaving to become Lord Mayor of Amsterdam

> Paint bladders and brush, said to have belonged to Rembrandt van Rijn

Design of a plaque bestowed on Pieter Jacob Six in recognition of his service to the resistance as Chief of the Public Order Commission during the Second World War, 1965

Immediately below it you can see a gilded silver tulip cup by J. Lutma. The cup was presented to the Guild of Surgeons by Dr Nicolaes Tulp, when he retired as President. Although the cup was subsequently stolen, it was re-acquired several years later by Jan Six II, who kept it as a memento of his grandfather. The central cabinet also contains two green-coloured Delft sauce bowls and a 'Bolshevik' cut diamond, set in a man's ring given by Tsar Alexander I in 1814.

The middle shelf of the cabinet on the far right holds a collection of coconut cups. The bottom shelf contains paint bladders, said to have belonged to Rembrandt van Rijn and a number of modern medals and decorations, among others the design of a plaque bestowed on Pieter Jacob Six in recognition of his service to the resistance as Chief of the Public Order

Commission during the Second World War. Also visible is a small portrait of Nine Six-Bosch Reitz, painted on the occasion of the 80th birthday.

The lacquer box is by a contemporary Russian artist and shows my wife Annabelle Dresselhuys and myself, wearing garments belonging to our forefathers. It was given to us as a token of appreciation for our help in establishing the 'Cat Cabinet' (*Katten-kabinet*), a museum that specialises in painted felines (established 1990).

The library contains over 100,000 documents and books about the Six family and its relations, covering a period of 1,000 years. Among them are letters from Joost van den Vondel, George Washington, the Marquis de Lafayette and the German Emperor Wilhelm II. The statue downstairs is of the Roman emperor Agrippa and dates back to around 20 B.C.

Finally, you will find the guest book at the front door. The latest of over 20 volumes that have been signed by friends, guests and visitors since 1652. By leaving their name, guests to the House of Six continue to build this small monument dedicated to my family. Please make your contribution to this record of the past, present and future for which I, on behalf of my ancestors, am very grateful.

Charter, given by King Charles II of England, one among the 100,000 documents and books about the Six family and its history

The staircase was contructed by Ignatius van Locheren in 1725.

The bookcase containing all publications written by Jan Six VII

The marble statue of Emperor Agrippa dating back to the Roman Empire

FAMILY TREE IN DIRECT LINE

Jean Six
(1575-1617)

Jan Six, Lord of Wimmenum and Vromade
(1618-1700)

Jan Six, Lord of Hillegom and Vromade
(1668-1750)

Jan Six, Lord of Hillegom, Wimmenum and Vromade
(1730-1779)

Mr Jan Six, Lord of Hillegom, Wimmenum and Vromade
(1756-1827)

Jan Six, Lord of Wimmenum and Vromade
(1788-1863)

Jhr Mr Hendrik Six, Lord of Hillegom
(1790-1847)

Jhr Jan Pieter Six, Lord of Hillegom and Vromade
(1824-1899)

Prof. Jhr Dr Jan Six, Lord of Hillegom and Wimmenum
(1857-1926)

Jhr Jan Six, Lord of Hillegom
(1891-1961)

Jhr Jan Six, Lord of Hillegom
(1919-1999)

Jhr Jan Six, Lord of Hillegom
(1947)

Jhr Jan Six
(1978)

Anna Wymer
(1584-1654)

Margaretha Tulp
(1634-1709)

Agatha Decquer
(1668-1693)
Maria Calkoen
(1674-1728)
Anna Elisabeth van den Bempden
(1695-1773)

Susanna Catharina Bors van Waveren
(1730-1760)
Johanna Clifford
(1733-1797)

Johanna Maria Hop
(1769-1809)
Anna Margaretha Cornelia van Gelé Twent
(1782-1861)

Lucretia Johanna van Winter
(1785-1845)

Jkvr. Catharina Teding van Berkhout
(1834-1887)

Hieronyma Maria Antonia Fortunata Bosch Reitz
(1867-1951)

Christina Diederika van der Crab
(1892-1961)

Jkvr. Thecla Françoise van Styrum
(1923)
Anne Margreet van Krimpen
(1935)

Annabelle Dresselhuys
(1949)

Jhr Hendrik Bastiaan Six
(1980)

VI

VII

VIII

IX

X